# Skipper the Florida Dog

## *Adventure at the Marina*

Greg Dietrich

# Copyright

Copyright © 2010 by Greg Dietrich. 64293-DIET
Library of Congress Control Number: 2010909587

ISBN:
Softcover 978-1-917306-76-8
Hardcover 978-1-917306-77-5

All rights reserved. No part of this book may be reproduced or transmitted in any form or by any means, electronic or mechanical, including photocopying, recording, or by any information storage and retrieval system, without permission in writing from the copyright owner.

This is a work of fiction. Names, characters, places and incidents either are the product of the author's imagination or are used fictitiously, and any resemblance to any actual persons, living or dead, events, or locales is entirely coincidental.

This book was printed in the United States of America.

Illustrations by Lorena Birk
Edited by Gail Infanti

In memory of Skipper Donaldson

Dedicated to
Sarah, Mary Elizabeth, Jessica, Adam, Amy, Joliet, Lincoln, and Cole.
May your lives be full of adventure

The sun rises early over the coast of Florida. Skipper, a Golden Retriever, is awakened to the salty smell of the water and a warm breeze in his face.

Skipper lives on a boat in a marina with his master, an old fisherman named Sol. The marina is a wonderful place for a dog to live because there are so many fun things to do.

Today, Skipper has plans to go with his friend, Rusty, to chase Fiddler Crabs on the morning's low tide. Fiddler Crabs live in small holes in the sand near the water's edge. One of the crab's claws is much bigger than the other making the crab look like it is carrying a fiddle.

As Skipper jumps off the boat, he sees his friend, Rusty, coming up the dock. Rusty is a short, wiry haired dog who lives on the boat next door. The two exchange greetings and head off on the way to their new adventure.

Along the way they run into another resident of the marina, a pelican named Gus.

Pelicans are birds that love to eat fish, and some say that Gus is by far the best fisherman at the marina. He flies over the water and, when he sees a fish, he dives into the water scooping it up into his large bill.

"What are you two doing today?" asked Gus. "We are going to chase Fiddler Crabs," said Rusty, as they ran past. "Don't catch them all," laughed Gus, knowing the crabs are almost impossible to catch.

Upon reaching the end of the dock, the two find a little stretch of beach. "There they are," says Rusty, spotting a group of crabs. "Let's go," yells Skipper, as they race after them.

Fiddler Crabs stay close to their holes in the sand which makes them very hard to catch. Skipper and Rusty love to chase the crabs even though they have never caught one.

However, there was one time a Fiddler Crab caught Skipper. He was looking into a crab's hole when the crab came out and grabbed him by the nose. Skipper remembers how much it hurt and he'll never let that happen again.

As Skipper and Rusty give chase, each crab would duck back into their hole at the last minute. "I almost had one," yelled Rusty, just missing a large crab that barely fit back into the small hole. "You'll get him next time," replied Skipper, after watching the close call. It was like a game of tag for Rusty and Skipper. However, they were always it and never stopped running.

It gets pretty hot under the Florida sun and, as time goes by, the two decided they needed a rest. They headed to their favorite break spot, a large pine tree that sits on a hill overlooking the marina.

In the cool shade of the tall pine, they soon fall asleep. Skipper and Rusty spend the rest of the afternoon dreaming about the many adventures they had playing around the marina.

Suddenly, the two were awakened to the sound of a large flock of birds making a terrible racket. Looking out over the bay, they could see the fishing fleet returning from their daily trip.

Most of the boats at the marina are commercial fishing boats. Commercial fisherman, like Sol, make a living catching fish. They sell their catch to seafood markets for everyone to enjoy.

Skipper could hardly wait for his master and the rest of the fishing fleet to return. A crowd always gathers to greet the fisherman and see the many different kinds of fish caught that day.

Cleaning and throwing the remains of the fish back into the water always attracts a lot of birds including Gus, the pelican. Gus usually catches his own fish; however, because he is getting older, he is always eager for an easy meal.

When the last fish is cleaned, the crew starts washing down the boats. Skipper and Rusty know it is time to call it a day.

Heading back down the dock tired and hungry, they are both happy to see dinner waiting for them.

After dinner, Skipper sat on the deck watching the sun set. He felt happy to live in such a wonderful place. With the smell of the water and a breeze in his face, he happily looks forward to his next adventure at the marina with his friend, Rusty.

THE END

www.ingramcontent.com/pod-product-compliance
Lightning Source LLC
Chambersburg PA
CBHW040023130526
44590CB00036B/79